Citizen Scientist

STUDYING

POLLUTION

IZZI HOWELL

WAYLAND
www.waylandbooks.co.uk

First published in Great Britain in 2020 by Wayland

Produced for Wayland by
White-Thomson Publishing Ltd
www.wtpub.co.uk

Series Editor: Izzi Howell
Designer: Clare Nicholas

HB ISBN: 978 1 5263 1224 2
PB ISBN: 978 1 5263 1225 9
10 9 8 7 6 5 4 3 2 1

MIX
Paper from
responsible sources
FSC® C104740
FSC
www.fsc.org

Wayland
An imprint of
Hachette Children's Group
Part of Hodder & Stoughton
Carmelite House
50 Victoria Embankment
London EC4Y 0DZ

An Hachette UK Company
www.hachette.co.uk
www.hachettechildrens.co.uk

Printed in China

Picture acknowledgements:
Shutterstock: SmallSnail cover top, Oceloti cover centre, Iconic Bestiary cover bottom left, Andres_Aneiros cover bottom right, BlueRingMedia title page and 4, Pretty Vectors 2, Supriya07 3t, 5t and 30t, MaryValery 3c and 7, Crystal Eye Studio 3b, 24 and 30b, VectorPlotnikoff 5c and 8t, Kastoluza 5b, Iconic Bestiary, MSSA and alazur 6t, Zefir 6cl, brown32 6cr, robuart 6b, Arcady 8b, Olha1981 9t, Igogosha 9bl, Sergey Mastepanov 9br, MuchMania 10–11b, filkusto, Luis Molinero, Studio_G, Rvector and Alla_vector 10, VicW 11t, Panptys 11b, trgrowth 12l, Oceloti 12r, jkcDesign 13t, HP30 13bl, Maria_OH 13br, robuart, Rvector, pikepicture and Volosovich Igor 14, Nygraphic 15, Golden Sikorka 16t, Kapreski 16c, Inspiring 16b, Arcady 17t, Adrian Niederhaeuser 17c, VVadyab Pico 17b, Vector Plus Image 18, kuroksta 19t, gritsalak karalak 19c, Marnikus 19b, grmarc 20t, Ku_suriuri 20b, Business stock 21t, JamesPlay 21cl, Faber14 21cr, Panaiotidi 21b, Techtype 22, DreamCold 23t, Vector FX 23b, Sergey Yukhnovets 25t, brown32 25b, Fancy Tapis 26t, Julia Zova, Vector Tradition, uiliaaa, petrroudny43, BlueRingMedia and Oleh Markov 26c, lineartestpilot 26b, Viktorija Reuta 27t, Nadzin 27b, mapush 28, Doloves 29t, Ysami 29b.

All design elements from Shutterstock.

CONTENTS

CITIZEN SCIENCE AND POLLUTION

Citizen science is a way to help out with scientific research across the world, by taking part in observations and submitting data. Working as citizen scientists, we can observe pollution to see how it affects natural habitats and help to reduce it.

WHAT IS POLLUTION?

Pollution is damage done to the environment caused by harmful substances. Humans create air pollution, water pollution and soil pollution by throwing away rubbish and by dumping chemicals and other damaging materials. High levels of noise and light generated by human activity also create pollution that affects the health of humans and wildlife.

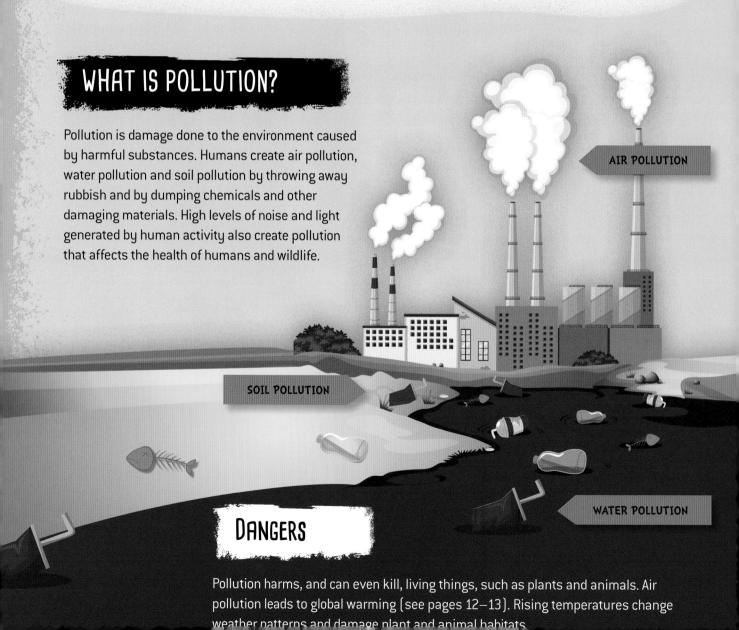

AIR POLLUTION

SOIL POLLUTION

WATER POLLUTION

DANGERS

Pollution harms, and can even kill, living things, such as plants and animals. Air pollution leads to global warming (see pages 12–13). Rising temperatures change weather patterns and damage plant and animal habitats.

Plastic pollution kills more than

1 MILLION

seabirds every year.

TIME TO ACT

For most of human history, our population was much smaller and had less impact on the natural world. We didn't throw away plastic, drive vehicles or use power plants to generate electricity. In the past 100 years or so, human activity has started to seriously harm the environment. Time is running out – we need to act now to help prevent further climate change, save plant and animal species, and reduce the risk to human health.

SOLVING THE PROBLEM

Big companies are mainly responsible for the pollution that creates huge environmental problems, such as the production of greenhouse gases (see pages 12–13). However, we can all do our bit to help by making small changes, such as walking or cycling instead of driving. Get involved with environmental campaigns in your local area and take part in citizen science projects to gather useful data about pollution.

RUBBISH ROUND-UP

PROJECT

Many places in your local area may be polluted with rubbish. Go on a rubbish round-up and find data to confirm which place has the most pollution.

Choose four places in your local area, such as your school playground, a park, a bus stop, a street near a cafe, a street near a supermarket, a beach or a stream. Go with an adult and be very careful near roads and water.

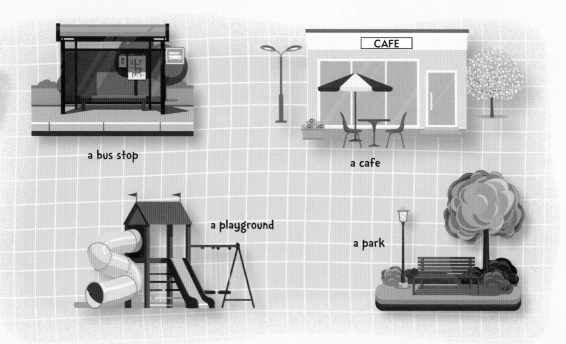

a bus stop

a cafe

a playground

a park

Choose an amount of time to spend collecting rubbish, for example 15 minutes. Spend this amount of time picking up rubbish in each location. Wear gardening gloves to protect your hands or use a rubbish picker. Do not pick up anything sharp, such as broken glass.

Collect the rubbish from each location in a different bag. When you've finished, take the bags home and weigh each bag on a set of scales. Which location has the most rubbish? Why do you think that is?

Once you have finished, present your data in a pie chart to show which location has the most rubbish.

Location	Weight of rubbish collected (kg)
Outside supermarket	4
Park	1.9
School playground	2.5
My street	0.8

First, copy your data into a spreadsheet in Excel. It should look something like this.

Then, select all of the cells that contain data and click the 'Charts' button. Choose the 'Pie' option. This will create a pie chart from your data. If you hold the mouse over each section of the chart, it will show you the per cent that each section represents of the total. For example, rubbish from outside the supermarket made up 43 per cent of all rubbish collected.

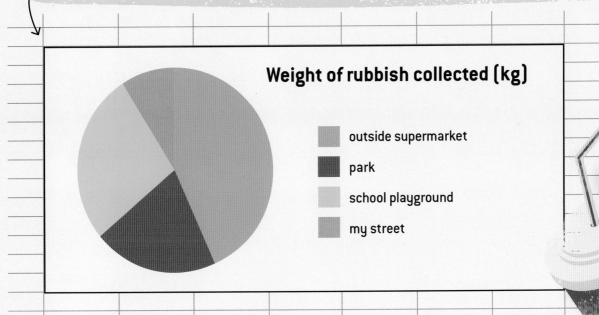

Weight of rubbish collected (kg)

- outside supermarket
- park
- school playground
- my street

GET INVOLVED!

Once you've found out which areas have the most rubbish, organise regular rubbish pick-ups to keep them cleaner. You could do this as part of a national campaign, such as the Great British Spring Clean.

AIR POLLUTION

Air pollution is a huge threat to the environment, harming plants, wildlife and human health.

SOURCES OF POLLUTION

Air pollution is released by factories, petrol- and diesel-powered vehicles, and power plants that burn fossil fuels (coal, oil and natural gas) to generate electricity. This air pollution is made up of greenhouse gases (see pages 12–13), tiny solid particles and toxic gases.

HEALTH PROBLEMS

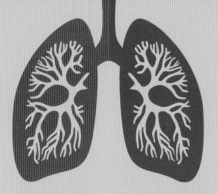

When we breathe in the tiny particles in air pollution, they can cause breathing problems or trigger allergies. They travel inside the body, causing asthma, lung disease and even cancer.

4.2 MILLION people die every year as a result of health issues linked to air pollution.

Acid rain

Sulphur dioxide and nitrogen oxides are substances released as air pollution from factories and vehicle exhausts. They mix with water and oxygen in the air to create acid. This acid is carried by the wind and eventually falls to the ground as acid rain. Acid rain harms animals and plants and can even dissolve the rock on buildings.

Reducing air pollution

We can reduce air pollution by using clean sources of energy, such as solar, tidal and wind power. These sources of energy do not release air pollution. We can also reduce the number of cars on the road by using public transport or bicycles instead. Electric cars are also a good alternative, as they don't create exhaust fumes, though the electricity that powers them may come from fossil fuels.

MEASURE AIR POLLUTION

Tiny particles of pollution are released into the air by vehicles and factories. By trapping these particles you can test the levels of pollution in different locations, such as a park, a busy road or a school playground.

YOU WILL NEED:

A4 sheets of thick white card

Scissors

A ruler

Gridded paper

Glue

A hole punch

String

Petroleum jelly

A magnifying glass

/// WARNING ///
BE CAREFUL HANDLING SCISSORS

Cut the white card into four squares measuring 8 cm by 8 cm. Then, cut four 7 cm by 7 cm squares from the graph paper and stick one on to each card using glue. Punch a hole in the top of each card. Tie a piece of string through the hole in a loop for hanging.

Use your finger to spread a thin layer of petroleum jelly over the gridded paper on each card. Choose four different locations to hang your cards. You can hang them on tree branches or drawing pins. Label each card as a science experiment so that they aren't disturbed.

Leave the cards for 6 to 10 days (the same for all cards) and then collect them. Use the magnifying glass to count the number of particles. If there are lots of particles, just count the number of particles in one square in the grid, then multiply this result by the number of squares in the grid. Make a note of your results.

PROJECT

Once you've got your results, turn them into a bar chart using the Excel program. First, copy your data into a spreadsheet in Excel. It should look something like this.

Location	Number of particles
School playground	18
Pedestrian shopping street	26
Car park	45
Woodland	4

Then, select all of the cells that contain data and click the 'Charts' button. Choose the 'Bar' option. This will create a bar chart from your data.

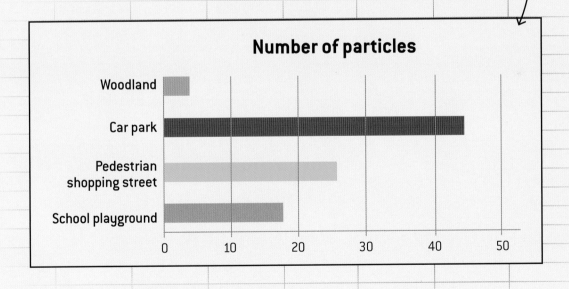

Number of particles

TRY IT!

Organise a Walk to School day to reduce pollution around your school. You could also join an international campaign to reduce air pollution, such as Breathelife by the World Health Organization.

GLOBAL WARMING

Gases released by industry and vehicles contribute to the greenhouse effect. This increases the temperature on Earth (global warming) and causes climate change.

atmosphere

greenhouse gases

heat

Sun

THE GREENHOUSE EFFECT

Greenhouse gases are gases such as carbon dioxide, water vapour, methane and nitrous oxide. When released, they gather in the atmosphere and trap heat from the Sun close to the surface of Earth.

NATURAL GASES

The greenhouse effect is natural. A low level of greenhouses gases in the atmosphere keeps Earth warm enough for living things to survive. Greenhouse gases are released naturally when humans and wildlife breathe and by volcanoes.

GLOBAL WARMING

Human activity, such as industry, farming and transport, releases large amounts of greenhouse gases into the atmosphere. This means that more heat is trapped close to Earth, as the layer of greenhouse gases is thicker. As a result, the average temperature on Earth is rising beyond what is normal. This can be slowed down if we act now and reduce the amount of greenhouse gases released.

The average temperature on Earth has risen by

0.9°C

since the late nineteenth century.

This doesn't sound like a lot, but it makes a huge difference.

CLIMATE CHANGE

Higher temperatures have a serious impact on natural habitats. Ice is melting at the poles, which destroys polar habitats. The melted ice goes into the oceans and makes sea levels rise around the world. Higher temperatures also lead to more extreme weather, such as storms, drought and floods.

CHANGING SEASONS

Warmer temperatures affect plants and animals. Flowers bloom and produce fruit earlier. Animals migrate at different times. This throws ecosystems out of balance, as food is not always available for animals at the correct time. Many animals can go hungry or die.

TEST THE GREENHOUSE EFFECT

Try this experiment on a sunny day to see how the greenhouse effect works. The cling film traps heat inside the jars, just like greenhouse gases do in the atmosphere.

YOU WILL NEED:

Two identical large glass jars

Two thermometers

Two strips of cardboard that will fit inside the jars

Sticky tape

A piece of cling film

A piece of white paper

Tape each thermometer to a strip of cardboard so that it will stand up. You may need to bend the bottom of the strip for balance. Place a thermometer in each of the jars. Cover the top of one of the jars in cling film. Make sure that it is completely covered. Leave the other jar open.

Place the jars on a piece of white paper in direct sunlight, such as a windowsill. Both jars should be exposed to an equal amount of sunlight. Take a reading of each thermometer as you start your experiment, and again every five minutes for one hour. If the Sun moves, move the jars so that the sunlight is always on them equally.

Once you have collected your data, present it in a line graph. The line goes up to show how the temperature changes over time.

Time (in minutes)	Jar 1 (no cling film) temperature in °C	Jar 2 (cling film) temperature in °C
0	16	16
5	16	16.5
10	16.5	17
15	16.5	17.5
20	17	18
25	17	19
30	17	19.5
35	17	20
40	17	20.5
45	17	21

First, copy your data into a spreadsheet in Excel. It should look something like this.

Then, select all of the cells that contain data and click the 'Charts' button. Choose the 'Line' option. This will create a line graph from your data.

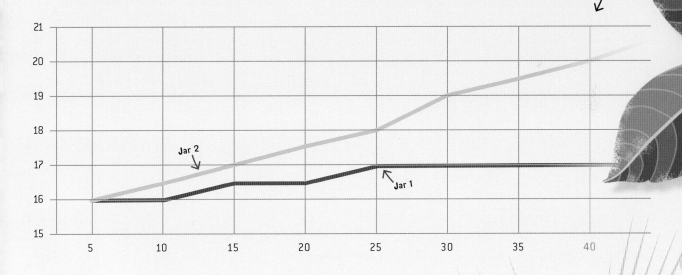

TRY IT! Try placing ice cubes of roughly the same size and weight in both jars. In which jar do they melt first? Instead of the Sun, you could use lamps for this experiment. Try controlling the amount of light on each jar. What happens if you use less or more light?

WATER POLLUTION

Water pollution affects aquatic animals and plants. If people's drinking water gets polluted, it can cause health problems or even death.

FACTORIES AND FARMS

Water can be polluted by chemicals, fertilisers and waste products from factories and farms. These substances are illegally dumped into rivers, lakes and the sea or washed into waterways by the rain. There, they poison aquatic plants and animals.

AN OCEAN DUMP

Plastic waste is dumped in the ocean or swept into the water by wind. Animals get trapped in large plastic items in the water. Some animals even eat small plastic items, thinking that they are food. This damages their internal organs and can kill them.

Every minute, ONE RUBBISH LORRY-LOAD of plastic is dumped into the oceans.

Oil spills

Oil rigs and cargo ships are sometimes damaged and spill oil into the oceans. The oil covers ocean birds and mammals. Oil-covered birds and mammals can't swim or maintain their body temperature, so they often drown or die from hypothermia. They also consume oil when they try to clean themselves, which poisons them.

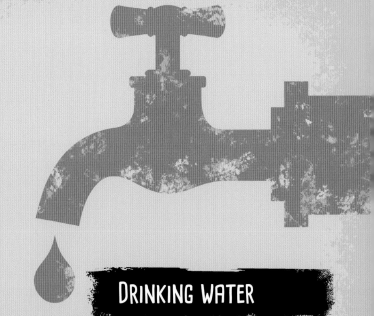

Drinking water

In some less economically developed countries, people have limited access to toilets or sanitation. Human waste is released directly into rivers and lakes. This polluted water is used for drinking water, if there are no other sources of treated drinking water that are safe to drink. People can catch diseases, such as cholera, and become ill.

Cleaning up

Reducing the amount of waste we produce (see pages 24–25) will decrease the quantity in the oceans. It's hard to collect waste that's already in the water, but we can clean up rubbish from beaches. We can also write letters and create petitions to put pressure on governments to control factories and farms and make them stop releasing chemicals into the water supply.

DISCOVER WATER pH

Find out if local water sources have been affected by pollution by testing their pH with litmus paper. Water is normally neutral, but it can become acidic or alkaline if it is polluted.

The pH scale is a measure of how acidic or alkaline a liquid is. Acids and alkalis are substances that contain chemicals that can cause damage. The pH scale goes from 0 to 14. The acidic levels are 0 to 6, 7 is neutral (neither acidic nor alkaline) and 8 to 14 is alkaline. The more acidic or alkaline a liquid is, the more it can damage other things. The pH of water affects the animals and plants that live in it.

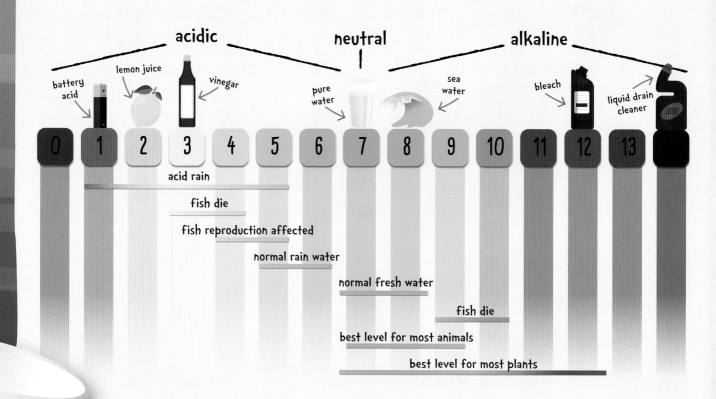

acidic   neutral   alkaline

battery acid — 0
lemon juice — 1
vinegar — 3
pure water — 7
sea water
bleach — 12
liquid drain cleaner

0 1 2 3 4 5 6 7 8 9 10 11 12 13

acid rain
fish die
fish reproduction affected
normal rain water
normal fresh water
fish die
best level for most animals
best level for most plants

YOU WILL NEED:

Litmus paper strips (can be bought online)

Three paper cups

Choose three fresh water sources in your local area, such as a stream, a lake or a pond. At each site, fill a paper cup roughly half full with water. Go with an adult and do not collect water from deep areas, fast-moving rivers or anywhere where you are at risk. Wash your hands afterwards.

Dip a strip of litmus paper into each cup of water. Follow the instructions on the packet to see how long to leave the litmus paper in. The paper will change colour depending on the pH of the water. The packet will include a colour guide for you to follow.

Depending on the brand of litmus paper, it will probably be red-orange if it is acidic, green if it is roughly neutral and blue if it is alkaline. If the litmus paper is red-orange or blue, the water has been polluted. When you have taken your three readings, compare your results. Which of the three sources has the best water for plant and animal life?

TRY IT!

Test leftover litmus strips on other water sources. Salt water is more alkaline than fresh water, so try testing it if you live near the sea. You could also test tap water or other household liquids, such as milk or washing up liquid.

NOISE AND LIGHT POLLUTION

Noise and light pollution may not seem as serious as other types of pollution, but they have a significant impact on animal behaviour and human health.

SOURCES OF NOISE

Noise pollution comes from factories, roads, airports, machinery and construction projects. Loud noises or repetitive noises cause the most damage. Noise pollution can happen on land and on water, as ships make a lot of noise.

ANIMALS

Excess noise creates stress for animals. This can make them leave their habitat, as they escape noisy areas to find quieter places to live. This has a knock-on effect across the ecosystem, as these animals may have been sources of food or predators of other animals. Noise pollution can also confuse animals that use sound to hunt or navigate, such as whales.

STRESS AND SLEEP

Noise also affects human health. It can increase stress levels and cause sleeping problems. Very loud noises can even lead to hearing loss.

SHHHHH!

To reduce noise pollution, the government can place noise restrictions on factories and construction projects. They can also ban the construction of new homes near busy, noisy areas, such as airports. Building walls along the sides of busy roads can help to block the sound of cars.

SOURCES OF LIGHT

Light pollution comes from homes, businesses and streetlights. It is caused by people leaving bright lights switched on all night. It mainly happens in towns and cities, where lots of small amounts of light pollution add up to create a big problem.

NIGHT OR DAY?

Light pollution confuses nocturnal animals, such as owls. As it never gets truly dark, these animals don't know when to come out and hunt for food. This affects the amount of food that they eat, which has a knock-on effect on their health.

LIGHTS OFF

The simplest way to prevent light pollution is by turning off unnecessary lights. Some lights can also be put on a timer, so that they turn off automatically, or used with a sensor, so that they only turn on when people walk past. All of these strategies will also help to save electricity.

CHECK LIGHT POLLUTION

Measure how much light pollution there is in an area by spotting objects in the night sky and using the Bortle scale, which measures the sky's brightness.

This diagram shows the different levels of the Bortle scale.

8/9 City sky
- The whole sky is brightly lit and whitish grey.
- Very few stars can be seen.
- The Moon is one of the only things that can be seen.

6 Bright suburban sky
- The sky is grey towards the horizon.
- Some stars can be seen.

4 Rural/suburban sky
- Traces of the Milky Way galaxy can be seen.

1/2 Dark site
- Zodiacal light (triangular white glow stretching up from the horizon) is visible.

7 Suburban/city sky
- The sky has a light grey colour.
- A few stars can be seen weakly.

5 Suburban sky
- More stars can be seen.

3 Rural sky
- The Milky Way galaxy can be seen clearly.

Use the Bortle scale to test light pollution in your local area. Go out with an adult at night and take a look at the night sky. What colour is the sky? Which stars can you see? Use this information to place your location on the scale.

If you go to another area that is different to your home location, such as the countryside if you live in the city, repeat the experiment. What can you see? How does this new place score on the Bortle scale?

Here are two of the most common constellations (star patterns) in the night sky. You'll see different constellations at different times of year, depending on where you live. Why not keep track of the constellations that you see and record how they change over the year?

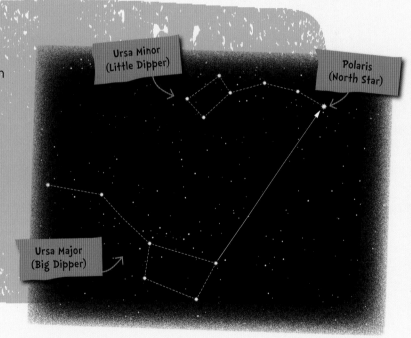

Ursa Minor (Little Dipper)

Polaris (North Star)

Ursa Major (Big Dipper)

TRY IT!

There are mobile phone apps that can measure light pollution. On iPhones, try the Dark Sky Meter app. You can upload and share your results on the Dark Sky Meter website to create an atlas of light pollution across the world. For Android phones, the Loss of the Night app can also measure light pollution. Check with an adult before downloading any apps.

RUBBISH AND RECYCLING

It can be easy to ignore what happens to rubbish after we throw it away. However, many things that we discard create pollution and harm the environment.

BIN TO LANDFILL

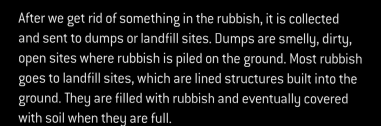

After we get rid of something in the rubbish, it is collected and sent to dumps or landfill sites. Dumps are smelly, dirty, open sites where rubbish is piled on the ground. Most rubbish goes to landfill sites, which are lined structures built into the ground. They are filled with rubbish and eventually covered with soil when they are full.

Around the world, nearly **1 million plastic bottles** are bought every minute.

BREAKING DOWN

Most of the rubbish sent to landfill will take hundreds or even thousands of years to decompose (break down). As we throw away more and more rubbish over time, it will take up huge amounts of space. Eventually, we will run out of space for landfill sites. Rubbish in landfill sites can also release chemicals that pollute the soil and poison plants and animals.

REDUCE AND REUSE

The best way to reduce the amount of rubbish that goes to landfill is to cut down on the amount of rubbish we create. The best solution is to buy less. Look for sustainable solutions, such as reusable water bottles or lunchboxes, rather than using disposable containers. Reuse things before throwing them away, for example, by using scrap paper for writing. Give unwanted items to a charity shop so that someone else can use them.

This diagram shows the best order of dealing with waste.

REDUCE
REUSE
RECYCLE
LANDFILL

Most sustainable

Least sustainable

RECYCLING

As well as reducing the number of items you use, recycling old items is a good option. Many items can be recycled, such as glass, tins, paper, cardboard and some types of plastic. Recycling stops items from going to landfill and means that resources do not need to be used to make new items. However, it does require energy to recycle old items, which is why reducing and reusing is preferable.

COMPOST

Organic waste, such as leftover food or food scraps, decomposes quickly into compost. This compost can be used to grow fruit and vegetables or plants and flowers. Many towns and cities offer an organic waste collection service, so you don't need a compost bin to recycle your organic waste.

WILL IT BIODEGRADE?

Test which materials are biodegradable and will break down into soil. Can you guess which ones will break down the most in only two weeks?

YOU WILL NEED:

Gardening gloves

A trowel

1 cm x 1 cm pieces of:
- cardboard
- cotton fabric
- lettuce
- plastic shopping bag
- biodegradable shopping bag
- tin foil
- newspaper

A place marker

A sheet of graph paper with a 5 mm x 5 mm grid

A pencil

THE NEWS

Find a place for your experiment. It could be in a garden, an area of the school playground or an allotment. Check for permission from the person in charge of the land.

Wearing gardening gloves, dig a 30 cm x 30 cm hole about 4 cm deep. Place the pieces of material in the hole. Make sure that they are not touching each other. Cover the pieces in soil. Use the place marker to label the spot of your experiment so that you can find it again later.

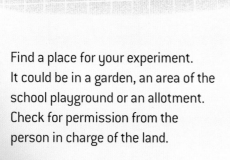

You could also do the experiment in flowerpots filled with soil, but you will need to water them every few days or leave them outside in the rain.

After two weeks, dig up your materials. Carefully remove each one from the soil and place them on the graph paper. Trace around each of the materials. Colour in the shape and label it. Count how many squares it takes up on the graph paper and write down your results in a table.

Material	Size before	Size after
Cardboard	4	3.5
Cotton fabric	4	3.7
Lettuce	4	2
Plastic shopping bag	4	4
Biodegradable shopping bag	4	3.5
Tin foil	4	4
Newspaper	4	2

Before the experiment, all the materials measured 1 cm x 1 cm, so they took up 4 squares.

TRY IT!

Repeat the experiment with other materials — some that you think will biodegrade and some that you think won't. Try leaving the materials for longer. How does this change your results? Don't use anything that will pollute the soil, such as washing tablets.

GET INVOLVED!

See if you can set up a compost bin in your garden or at school. You could use the compost to help grow fruit, vegetables and flowers.

KEEP IT FAIR

All of the projects in this book will help you to test pollution in your local area and get involved with helping to clean it up. However, it's important for you to make your experiments fair. If you don't control the different elements of an experiment, the results won't be accurate.

To change	To stay the same
The location	The size of the piece of card
	The amount of petroleum jelly
	The amount of time left outside

VARIABLES

There are lots of elements in experiments. These are called the variables. To make an experiment a fair test, you can only change one variable. All other variables have to stay the same. For example, in the air pollution project on pages 10–11, the only variable you are changing is the location. Everything else should stay the same.

INACCURATE RESULTS

If you have more than one variable, you won't know which one has affected your results. For example, if you used a larger piece of card, you wouldn't know if the high number of particles was because of the size of the card or because of the pollution levels. This makes your research inaccurate.

PLAN AHEAD

It's important to plan how you will make your experiment fair before you begin. This helps to keep the variables the same throughout. Write down important details, such as lengths of time, so that you don't forget.

OVER TO YOU!

When you've finished the projects in this book, why not make up your own?

First, you need to think of an idea that you want to test. This is called the hypothesis. For example,

'I THINK THAT AREAS WITHOUT BINS WILL HAVE MORE RUBBISH ON THE GROUND.'

Next, think about your variables — what will you keep the same and what will you change?

Then, carry out your experiment. You should repeat it a few times to make sure that your results aren't a one-off. This makes your results more reliable. Present your ideas using one of the graphs from the book. Finally, use your results to come up with a conclusion — what do the results show you? Was your hypothesis right or wrong?

GLOSSARY

atmosphere the layer of gases around Earth

biodegradable describes something that breaks down naturally and quickly without harming the soil

conclusion the judgement you reach after finding out all of the information necessary

decompose to break down and become soil

drought a period of time when there isn't enough water

ecosystem all of the living things in an area

fertiliser a substance placed on the soil to make plants grow well

fossil fuel a fuel that comes from the ground, such as coal, oil or gas

global warming the increase of the average temperature on Earth

greenhouse gas a gas that traps heat in the atmosphere, such as carbon dioxide

hypothermia a serious illness caused by being too cold

hypothesis an idea that needs to be tested

landfill a place where rubbish is buried in the ground

migrate to travel to a different place when the season changes

nocturnal describes an animal that is active at night

pH scale a scale that measure how acidic or alkaline a liquid is

substance a solid, liquid or gas

sustainable describes something that doesn't damage the environment so it can continue to be used for a long time

toxic poisonous

variable an element in an experiment that can change

BOOKS

Global Pollution *Our World in Crisis*
by Rachel Minay
Franklin Watts, 2018

Pollution *Ecographics*
by Izzi Howell
Franklin Watts, 2019

Plastic Planet
by Georgia Amson-Bradshaw
Franklin Watts, 2019

WEBSITES

www.wwf.org.uk/updates/ten-tips-reduce-your-plastic-footprint
Get ten tips to reduce the amount of plastic you use.

climatekids.nasa.gov/air-pollution
Learn more about air pollution.

www.theworldcounts.com/stories/What_is_Pollution_for_Kids
Find up-to-date information about the amount of pollution created so far this year.

INDEX

Citizen Scientist

STUDYING BIRDS

STUDYING INSECTS

STUDYING PLANTS

STUDYING POLLUTION